5 ANGLES

The Practical Fundamentals Of The World Of Filipino

Martial Arts Of Escrima, Arnis, & Kali

Frank Delo Jr.

Copyright Page:

5 Angles: The Practical Gateway Fundamentals To The World Of Filipino Martial Arts Of Escrima, Arnis, & Kali

© Copyright <<Dec 27, 2021>> Frank Delo Jr.

professional judgment of a health care or mental health care professional.

Neither the author nor the publisher can be held responsible for the use of the information provided within this book. Please always consult a trained professional before making any decision regarding treatment of yourself or others.

For more information, email AmalgamMartialAcademy@gmail.com.

ISBN: 979-8-9855227-1-6 (Paperback)

ISBN: 979-8-9855227-2-3 (Hardcover)

ISBN: 979-8-9855227-0-9 (eBook)

Table of Contents:

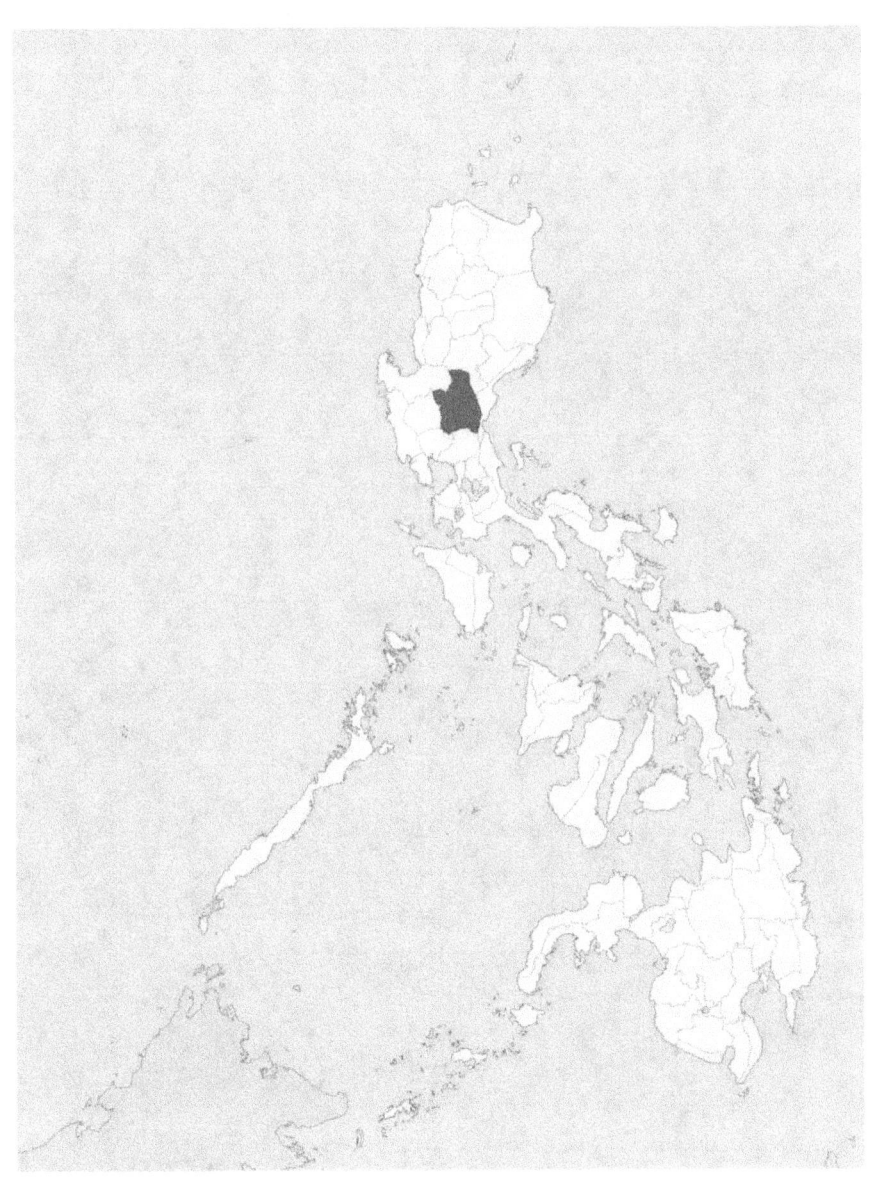

Nueva Ecija Province

INTRODUCTION

Salute. Welcome!

The world was a markedly different place when I started my personal martial arts journey back in the late 20th century. The internet as we know it was just barely on the verge of public release. The primary resources available to the martial arts enthusiast of the day were limited to the local Taekwondo or "karate" school. Research material was mostly available in print magazines and the occasional book in the local public library. Many of us struggled a great deal to find and gain new martial knowledge of real quality. Often, information was fragmented or otherwise incomplete due to circumstance, the whims of a particular teacher, or generations of the endless "telephone game" of exaggerated legends and oral traditions.

The Philippines has been a cultural melting pot for centuries. Elements from multiple countries in both the East and the West combined in a unique way in our little cluster of islands in the Pacific. Our language, customs, foods, and yes, even our martial arts are the result of generations of friendly and less friendly exchanges among people from all over the globe. The result, at least in a martial arts context, is one of the most internationally celebrated and practiced systems in existence. Elements of the Filipino martial arts are in use by professional protectors around the world, in the elite military forces and law enforcement agencies of nations across the globe, and featured in some of the most exciting works of international cinema. It's no wonder that at this point in time the Filipino martial arts are more popular and sought-after than at any time in history.

To date, there are many different subsystems of the Filipino martial arts. These include regional, ethnic, and, like my own system, family variants. For the new student interested in Filipino martial arts, there is no better time to begin your study. That said, the abundance of systems can be intimidating. What system should I begin studying? Is one system better than another? Are there "right or wrong" systems? What about "authenticity?" With thousands and thousands of videos freely available on YouTube and social media platforms, the new student to the Filipino martial arts can get overwhelmed in the sea of questionable material without a little guidance.

Writing this in the first half of the 21st century, we not only have many of the same problems as the last century, but we now have a new and unique problem: an overabundance of information. We have certainly benefited from this condition. If I want to research Filipino martial arts, there are thousands of search results in text, video, and audio formats on any number of online platforms. The problem, then, is quality. What's "authentic?" What's practical? What's going to get me put in jail or in the morgue?

Through time and training I've encountered another issue: experts don't know how to talk to beginners! Often the people who have struggled to earn high quality information get stuck communicating at their high levels of understanding, regardless of their audience. If you're not already an expert on the topic, a great deal of value can often sail over people's heads, going largely unappreciated. I've experienced this myself at seminars, where an esteemed guest teacher has a limited time to share as much value as possible, usually leaving people like me in the audience to digest the experience for days, weeks, or years until even a fraction of the value begins to be understood.

In this book, I am going to provide a quality resource against which beginners may measure their flood of information. I am also going to provide teachers an example of how to distill and communicate their wealth of knowledge to a novice audience in a practical, broadly accessible way. While serving both student and teacher, I will show you the core principles and foundational techniques of my family's Filipino martial art system.

I will freely admit here that I do not have all the answers. What I do have is my lifetime of training and experience in my family's system, the lessons I have learned from my colleagues and friends in their respective systems, my years of experience as a teacher both in a classroom setting and on the mats, and a sincere desire to help anyone who cares to listen to me with their personal pursuit of the world of Filipino martial arts.

I grew up learning my family's system of Filipino martial arts. My first teacher was my dad, who was not immediately forthcoming with the fact that he was actually teaching me a martial art. Until I was older, it made no difference to me. We were just sword fighting for fun as far as I knew. He would tell me stories of his father Silvino, my grandfather, defeating challengers as they occasionally visited their village ("barrio" or "barangay") of Baloy. For you geography nerds, Baloy is a barangay in the municipality of Cuyapo, in the province of Nueva Ecija in central Luzon island. Stories about relatives having fought in the many different conflicts of the history of the Philippines went as far back as the Spanish occupation. Some of those stories crossed over into my father's music education, where Grandpa would remind Dad of the wrong notes he played on his guitar via a sharp

4

notification with the end of his violin bow. (This was likely an angle one or two strike. We'll explore that later!).

As I grew older I trained in Taekwondo and explored the world of kobudo weapons introduced to me by such luminary masters as the Teenage Mutant Ninja Turtles and the many American ninja movies. As I went on to study music and my interests in damaging my hands began to decline, my martial interests led me to Chinese martial arts, and the Chinese internal arts in particular (bagua, tai chi etc.), which I continue to practice. The martial arts magazines I often consumed led me back to rediscover the Filipino martial arts. Upon showing Dad some of the articles and video learning ads in the magazines, many using Tagalog terms with which I was unfamiliar, he would just laugh and say, "That's just the games we used to play."

Many of the unfamiliar terms he told me were just simple terms like "boxing" or "weaving", helping to demystify what I was seeing and to work past the marketing. Regarding the many styles I began to see emerge, he reminded me that Filipino martial arts did not traditionally operate the same way as Japanese or Korean Arts, where teachers and students were beholden to preserving and promoting a set system. He said that often material was trained and shared within communities or individual families, each creating a unique identity for themselves. There are plenty of other books and resources regarding the history of Filipino martial arts, so I won't continue at length about that. I just want to share what I heard from Dad on the topic.

The longer I trained and the more teachers I interacted with, the more I began to identify the same elements I grew up with. When I attended a weekend FMA seminar with a prominent martial arts teacher only to discover that the fundamental movements and concepts were virtually identical to what I learned as a boy, I decided to go back to the source and learn from Dad in earnest.

And now here we are! My perspective as an adult martial artist and an experienced classroom teacher will help you engage with the whole world of Filipino martial arts in an accessible and understandable way, whatever level of experience you may have. Together we'll peel back the onion and look past the abundance of exercises and drills. You will see the fundamental principles at the core of all Filipino martial arts so that you can make your training more immediately practical.

I've used this information to help new students become competent enough with Filipino martial arts in their first few months of training to join and sometimes even win competitions. These are the principles that have shed light on years of training for some people, helping shift their knowledge from performance to combat practical almost overnight. Of course I can't guarantee overnight success for everyone. But, with careful, critical thought and consistent, quality practice, this book will definitely help you improve.

Chances are you have spent your share of hours stumbling around in the dark, sifting through dubious information from shady sources. You have wasted enough time. Dig into this book! Let's get right to the heart of things and make your Filipino martial arts practice really *work*.

Frank Delo Jr. & Frank Delo Sr.

General Concepts

Cinco Teros: Five Angles

Our system is "Cinco Teros" or "five angles." Variations exist across many systems. Here I will simply share the material as I received it. Most weapons systems, regardless of origin, organize information via a numbered angle system of some type — for example, the numbers around a clock. I've seen variants with up to 12 angles or more, with unique specific responses for each angle, and not always organized as intuitively as a clock. In our Cinco teros system, information is organized into four quadrants and a centerline, which is considered angle five. Offensive and defensive responses are more generalized and can be applied across the different angles.

Through working with different learners of all ages and backgrounds, I've found the five angles is a relatively easy way for people to organize and process information. We learn the angles at first by swinging a large X with the stick. The lines of the X pass through the four main quadrants and the point where they meet in the middle identifies the centerline. There are of course many other ways to engage all five angles, but the big X is the most simple and straightforward. Identifying the angles by their number helps organize the learning and practice.

Lateral Movement

Unlike some other martial arts that operate back and forth along single lines, in our system we prioritize lateral or sideways movement. Ideally we want to be in a spot that's harder for our opponent to attack us while also easier for us to attack or control our opponent in turn. Many other Filipino systems will teach their footwork concepts with a series of lines or triangles, organizing the terrain of an encounter in an intricate web of footsteps. Many traditional empty hand arts will even discuss the details of precisely how the feet should interact with the ground. This type of curriculum works for some, and it is important for the advancing student to understand the theory behind these things, but I know personally that's too much for me to process before I get frustrated. Footwork is part of a larger body of strategy. If we focus too quickly on complex patterns, structures, and concepts, students tend to get stuck.

Instead we start by establishing broad goals for the footwork. Am I about to get hit? Then let's use our feet to move ourselves to a safer spot! Is my opponent out of reach? Then let's use our feet to move ourselves to a better spot where we can hit them. Is my opponent trying to attack my legs? Let's use our feet to move those legs out of the way! Beyond that, we teach that when the hands move, the feet move. We don't like to stand still and trade blows. If my students are still getting tangled with this level of communication, I try to make it even more simple and tell them to keep their feet unglued from the floor regardless of what their hands are doing. This is very general, but it establishes important habits early on.

Witik: Quick Strikes

In our system we start with "witik" or quick strikes. Imagine the type of whipping motion you would use to whip somebody with a towel. I don't know how you grew up, but we used to do that to each other in the gym class locker room or around the pool. If you would prefer an image from a combat context, think about the jab. It's a quick harassing strike that sets the opponent up for bigger shots later on. The witik strike attacks quickly and immediately retreats. We do this for several reasons. Through continued play I'm sure you will discover even more.

An important concept through which we would apply this type of strike is the idea in most other Filipino martial arts systems of "defanging the snake." Simply put, we prioritize targeting the opponent's attacking limb, be it their weapon hand or whatever terrible appendage they may fling your way. Makes sense, right? They can't swing a weapon at you if they can't hold that weapon anymore. Beyond this, in our system when we can make the opportunity to go directly for the head. In a gruesome expansion of the defanging the snake concept, how can somebody continue their overall attack on us if we damage their central processing unit? Many of the stories I heard about Grandpa involved these quick headshots.

This is not to say that we don't teach big, powerful attacks where we follow through. Just like the jab is not the single, solitary technique in all of boxing, the witik lives in a larger body of strategy along with heavy decisive blows employed at strategic times. From a basic self-defense standpoint, the witik is easy to learn and employ almost regardless of a student's size, strength, or skill. A smaller-framed person attempting to fend off a physically larger attacker will simply never overpower that person, but with enough quick, accurate strikes, they may create enough space to escape to safety, which is the goal of self-defense in the first place.

Another example of this concept is the Chinese martial art of Wing Chun. Folklore States that the system was conceived by a woman to successfully defend herself from male attackers. Visually when compared to other Kung Fu systems, Wing Chun does not often employ large, whole-body swinging strikes and kicks. Instead, Wing Chun practitioners choose to focus on medium range, contact sensitivity, rapid techniques, and structural efficiency. While the execution may look different, these are all concepts valued in the Filipino martial arts as well. Perhaps this is why these arts often play well together and easily integrate together in people's individual martial practices.

Stick: Universal Analog

Our system is primarily a single stick system. We use the stick as an analog for any other weapon you could happen to pick up and employ. The movements are basically the same, but are adjusted based on the nature of the weapon. Again, this starts with swinging our big X from before, but from there we ask ourselves what the weapon is capable of. Can it strike, cut, stab, or control? What's the length and range? How can it be oriented in my grip? This makes students have to think carefully and critically about what they're holding and what they're doing.

11

Other systems may treat the different weapons more separately, prioritizing single stick or double stick, long blade or short blades, or some mix of each. This may even include empty-hand striking and grappling. For us, it's easier for the students to learn the same basic body of movement and to adjust the small details based on the weapon they're holding. I'll add here that our family system does not originally include any exclusive grappling material, to my knowledge. However, Dad is also a black belt in judo and karate, something of an early pioneer of mixing martial arts systems, in his small slice of the world at least. You can do what you want with that information.

The long leading end of the stick is used for striking, with a few fingers worth of stick protruding from the bottom. (More on that later.) It is also an analog for medium length blades like machetes or the revered and mysterious Filipino machete, the bolo knife In all its regional variations and flavors. But what about long swords, spears, axes, and many other diverse weapons? What about the awesome and terrifying Japanese katana? What about the broadsword-wielding ancient barbarian I'm supposed to fight on a neon-lit New York rooftop for the Ultimate Prize? I promise you, the stick and the basic movements will help get you where you need to be.

Change: Fluidity & Adaptability

This is an important concept for any martial artist, but we trained specifically for this in our system. No violent encounter will play out like a mathematical equation. We can structure our training and rehearse drills to impart responses, but ultimately if we are called upon to protect ourselves, we will need to get out of our own way and do what it takes to return to safety. This is partly why our information is organized broadly into five angles and why we tend to focus on principles versus specific movement or technique at first. Violent encounters are unpredictable, and under stress our bodies will be swirling with a cocktail of chemicals meant to help you survive. You will likely not be able to pull off anything terribly complex or cool-looking under those conditions. If you are pre-programmed with an effective general base of responses, your chances of survival will tip a little higher.

Like many other systems, Filipino or otherwise, we start with organized drills and repetitive patterns to start the mental and physical programming. Once a student has developed enough comfort with the basics, we start to apply more stress. We can throw in a random angle to an otherwise set drill, do the same drills with unfamiliar or mismatched weapons (stick vs knife, forward grip vs reverse grip, right vs left hands, or armed vs unarmed), and of course free sparring with mutually agreed upon levels of intensity. I will add here that while we value non-cooperative stress training, we generally don't do a lot of full-speed, full-contact fighting as part of our regular practice. Most of my students at the moment are not training for high-risk careers in military, law enforcement, or private security. Their day jobs or daily lives would not be greatly improved by six-inch stick welts or hairline fractures in their fingers, arms, collar bones, etc. If you believe I am being disingenuous by not training somebody's grandma or grandpa as if they're going to fight in a life-or-death pit battle with weapons, you may certainly continue believing that. I will certainly continue to do what I choose, and continue living life quite happily without caring about your opinion.

These broad points are the fundamentals of our system, and the core of what makes it work. If you are studying any other system of Filipino martial arts or any other martial art in general, these ideas may help make elements of your practice less confusing and possibly more effective. Either way, I hope it helps you on your martial journey. From here we will delve into the details of the system and its specific movements. If you find yourself confused at any point, return to this portion of the book and look back to the broad fundamental principles.

Example: Basic Sinawali Weaving Pattern

CINCO TEROS: THE FIVE ANGLES

In our system we see the world in terms of four quadrants and a centerline. Whether in terms of attack or defense, the majority of movements fall within a high line or low line, and to one side or the other of a vertical centerline. Seeing the world in these general zones helps simplify our choices of response. Without this layer of general organization, we are left trying to memorize potentially endless responses to individual attacks from potentially any direction. Some systems start teaching this way, providing specific attacks and responses at specific target points. As a student advances in these systems, the broader zones of response are implied and ingrained. The short answer is that these are different paths to the same destination.

The issue students tend to encounter when studying from specific to general like that is that violence itself is mostly unpredictable. A newcomer to self-defense and martial arts may be equipped with the handful of responses they learned from a quality teacher, but if they encounter an attack that is unfamiliar, something that falls outside the boundaries of their training, they are left to try to adapt quickly under stress. Depending on the individual student, this may or may not be successful for them.

However, when we begin our learning with general responses, that adaptability is tested immediately. Fluid adaptability is an attribute that is trained and developed immediately. Responses that fall within the loosely organized five angles may and should be adapted to any

33

mild variation within those areas. While in one system you may encounter five or six different responses from the crown of the head down to the opponent's left shoulder, in Cinco Teros that all falls within angle one. This is not to say that other systems are wrong. On the contrary, it is these systems and beyond that we should look towards to deepen and expand our understanding of principles and possibilities. But from the standpoint of immediate self-defense value, new students tend to benefit quickly from a practice focused primarily on the general.

Given that we see the world in four quadrants and a centerline, our opponents' attacks will travel towards us invariably through one of those zones. When we respond with our own weapon, we will invariably travel through one of those zones as well. Our first basic generic practice to become accustomed to these zones is to swing the stick in a simple "X" pattern. By tracing the lines of our X in either hand, both hands with double stick, even no hands, we get used to moving through these zones and begin to establish the gross motor movement that fuels our attacks and defenses. We swing that X solo and with a partner. This begins to establish our sense of distance, timing, and (when we keep our feet unglued) we begin to develop footwork and strategic position.

Angle 1

Angle 2

Angle 3

Angle 4

But if we're swinging the X, where is that fifth angle, the centerline? If you're paying close attention to your movement, the centerline is always at play. The middle of that X, where the lines cross, establishes the centerline. When opponents move to face each other, we orient naturally by our centerlines. Of course we do train to deal specifically with the centerline, via overhead strikes, various centerline thrusts, and the precious and sensitive groin. But just like the responses within a single quadrant are largely the same and can be quickly modified to cope with the unexpected, responses to angle five can be co-opted from effective responses from the other four angles.

Angle 5

The initial simplicity of our approach does not immediately reveal its potential depth or its infinite variations. But as I said, the beginning student is often best served by spending the most time in the realm of the general. Admittedly we do not have an endless list of curriculum. I would argue that if you have truly mastered your fundamentals, you do not need a lengthy curriculum to draw from. But if you are curious about how the fundamentals can play out, a lifetime of study awaits you in the broader world of Filipino martial arts and its many systems.

Basic Anatomical Targeting

Historically, all the stories Dad ever told me about Grandpa's village victories involve him targeting the weapon hand and the head of his opponents. There's a simple, efficient beauty about this idea, which is held by many other branches of Filipino martial arts, and other martial

45

systems and approaches to combat the world over. How could a man continue to attack you if the hand he attacks you with is decisively injured? Moreover, how can he continue attacking you, or even think of doing so, if his main computer is disrupted or turned off? The idea can be adjusted to the setting with relative ease and appropriate practice. In a defensive setting, these ideas can be trained in a way that potentially ends a violent encounter quickly with a minimum of physical harm. In more dire life or death settings, lethality is a close, though weighty capability.

In basic training patterns, we start by targeting our partner's stick. This helps us develop our timing and sense of range or distance. With adjustments to pace, equipment (gloves, pads, padded weapons, etc.), pressure, and an abundance of caution, we gradually train for our ultimate targets. Since most of my students are average peaceful citizens, we do our best to achieve honest, useful training while leaving them largely intact for their day jobs the next morning.

We say hand and head, but in reality even those specific terms are more broad. The idea of the attacking "hand" extends beyond the fingers and thumb to include the whole of an opponent's attacking limb and its constituent parts. While we can and do say to target, say, the gripping fingers, thumb, or the back of the hand, when other targets open up along the limb we can go for those as well. Areas like the wrist, forearm bones, the flexor tendons along the inner forearm, the muscles of the upper arm and shoulder... all can and should be considered effective targets.

Likewise we have an assortment of delicate and sensitive targets on the head, this being the main computer of the rest of the body. The sensory organs, eyes, ears, nose, and mouth, are all easily disrupted, even at a simple touch. Major bundles of blood vessels and nerves around the neck and sides of the skull are frighteningly accessible and close to the surface. And we shouldn't forget the simple, comical "bonk" on the head which, while not always a guaranteed knockout, is certainly always disruptive.

STANCE

We are not terribly particular about your stance. Simply stand upright and make sure you can move comfortably wherever you choose while keeping control of your balance. Wide stances make you less mobile, while narrow stances make it easy to fall (by accident or by design). Then again, longer ranges often call for larger stances and shorter ranges will in turn shrink stances. Be ready to flow and adapt!

Stance and footwork are always connected, one constantly morphing into the other. Usually Dad starts teaching this by stepping forward when he swings forward, and stepping back while he swings a backhand. This is a simple way to get used to the principle of "hands move feet move" as you begin your training and develop your limb independence.

GRIP

We grip the stick with a closed hammer grip. Simply open your hand and wrap fingers and thumb around the firm, girthy weapon of your choice in a secure fist. This allows you to manipulate the weapon as you need, while retaining the ability to punch with the weapon hand. You may see some other weapon arts open the bottom of the grip for the sake of accelerating spins or arcs. That can be done after a certain level of expertise, but generally we teach that any loosening of the grip is a possible opportunity for that weapon to leave your grip entirely.

This means that any circular movement of the weapon comes from the movement of the wrist, so warmups and training put attention towards wrist flexibility. We grip the stick towards one end with about two to three fingers worth of stick protruding from the bottom. This is the "punyo" or butt end of the stick. It leaves us enough stick at the bottom to employ techniques, but not quite enough stick for our opponent to grab and control effectively. The practice of this "butt stuff" transfers over to other areas like reverse grip knife, short defensive sticks like the "kubaton" and tactical pens, and the infamous and much chattered about online curvy claw of DEATH, the karambit (distant thunderclap).

STRIKES

As I said previously, our Cinco Teros system organizes information in four quadrants and a centerline. Whether armed or unarmed, striking in our system basically reduces down to forehand and backhand movement. Forehand strikes originate from the outer extremities of the body and move in towards the centerline, while backhand strikes originate from across the centerline and travel outward. This is regardless of which hand is moving. Even seemingly linear movements like stabs or straight punches tend to move from the outside in or from the inside out. Baguazhang, the other main martial system I train, is a predominantly circular and spiral oriented art. Movements are described as closing or opening, with the limbs rotating in or out in relation to one's centerline. I'm sure that practitioners of other systems will see the similarities and begin to connect the dots for themselves.

An important concept I tried to teach all of my students is that all the movements are largely the same. We simply adjust for the nature of the weapon. This means that a strike at angle one remains largely the same regardless of whether I'm swinging a stick, a machete, a small knife, an empty hand, or an elbow or other limb. All of these different weapons, of course, have different attributes and ranges, but the gross movements that drive them are largely the same. I have found through experience, at least with our body of students to this point, that focusing first on the larger movements and principles as opposed to

65

minute details of curriculum builds immediately practical self defense responses, and helps them build positive habits of mental flexibility under stress. This does not mean that systems with broad, deep, and complex curriculum are wrong. I'm simply saying that most new students, regardless of previous training, tend to learn better and develop deeper interests after effective fundamentals are established.

When I teach seminars, whether those seminars are for a corporate office or a gym full of experienced fighters, most students tend to be happier and more satisfied when they leave with some bit of practical, easy-to-remember information. These students also tend to be the ones who maintain contact and pursue further training. In contrast, whenever I get lost in the weeds chasing rabbit holes of theory or complex technique, 99% of the same body of students end up standing with eyes glazed over or glancing more frequently at the clock waiting for the next break.

That said, let's go back to our striking techniques. We start with a closed fist hammer grip around the bottom of the stick, with about two or three fingers worth of stick protruding from the bottom. The thoughtful teacher will point out to their students the potential of the simple grip around the basic stick. The longer end of the stick is an analog for any number of bladed weapons. The punyo, those couple inches of stick protruding from the bottom of your grip, is also an analog for any number of different weapons, but held in reverse grip. Even the grip, which is your sturdy closed fist, and by extension the rest of your arm, may be weaponized Into any number of punches and strikes. The larger mechanics remain the same, but the more we understand about the different weapons, the more we can adjust the smaller details of our technique to suit the use of those weapons.

As an aside, our system does not historically employ elements such as kicking or grappling to my knowledge. However, this does not mean we can't employ the broad principles of movement and striking or the ideas of five angles applied to these other skills. Kung fu has some useful ideas regarding this: "every step is a kick," and "the body is the fist." They hint at the fluidity of body usage within martial movement, and they bear some thoughtful consideration regardless of your martial art of choice. I would think twice about trying to head kick or grapple somebody with a machete, But the point remains. I encourage you to look at the broader principles and see where you can connect the dots.

Deflect & Intercept

Earlier we covered basic anatomical targeting, with the main goals being to target the hand and the head. The ideas of *deflect and intercept* begin to establish our choices of strategy. All of our physical contact with an opponent can be reduced down to these two categories. When we connect with an opponent's attack and pass or redirect it, we are deflecting. When we meet an opponent's force with force of our own like when we apply blocks or stop cuts, that is intercepting.

Each idea has its advantages and disadvantages. We start by learning to deflect. This can be initially frustrating since it takes some skill and coordination to do successfully. However the benefit is that it allows you to more easily manage attacks from a stronger, more powerful opponent. Regardless of what's coming in, if it is redirected away it no longer poses the same threat. And a good deflection with smart footwork puts you in a better position to counter and control the encounter.

Deflecting Angle 1

Deflect Angle 2

Deflect Angle 3

Deflecting Angle 4

Deflecting Angle 5

Our most natural response is to intercept or block incoming strikes. While it's natural, it's not always the safest choice. Anytime force goes against force, the more forceful opponent will gain advantage. A bigger, stronger opponent with a heavier weapon will generate a great amount of force. If you plan to block a strike from an opponent like that, you need to create a strong enough structure to bear the shock, and you need to follow up immediately with a decisive response to end the encounter quickly.

Another concern with blocking is that it tends to fix us in place. We tend to plant ourselves where we are and brace for impact, which leaves you in a danger zone longer. Whether we choose to deflect or intercept, we need to stay mobile and fluid to put ourselves in the best possible place.

Blocking Angle 1

Blocking Angle 2

Blocking Angle 3

Blocking Angle 4

Consecutive Contact

One of the overarching principles in Filipino martial arts is the idea of consecutive contact. While our family folklore has its share of stories of Grandpa ending fights in a single well-placed strike, it is the idea of consecutive contact that enables the practitioner to adapt and manage the flow of an encounter.

Example: Angle 4 Deflect & Counter

In other terms, this is the idea, taken from striking arts, of *throwing combinations*. Throwing more than one technique at a time can fulfill several goals during an encounter, from setup and strategy to simply dealing more damage at a time. Empty hand arts are used to this in the form of strikes and kicks. With Filipino martial arts, we add weapons into the mix. The family system is primarily single stick, so we often apply consecutive contact with one hand armed and the other empty. Like other popular systems, we also spend some time with a weapon in each hand. This can be in the form of double stick, where both hands are armed with weapons of equal length. It can also take the form of *espada y daga* (sword and dagger), or both hands armed with weapons of unequal length.

Example: Block & Pass Angle 1

The principle of *consecutive contact* applies regardless of armament. What changes are the nature and goals. I organize contact into two main categories, *attack and control.* A simple angle one swing can be either an attack or control, depending on the circumstances. If that angle one swing hits someone in the temple or collarbone, we could call it an attack. If that angle one swing is thrown in response to an opponent's attack, it can be considered a control, either blocking or redirecting the opponent's blow.

Consecutive contact can be a mix of each of these. Basic "sinawali" or weaving drills, and drills like "hubud," can be an example of consecutive controls, because both partners simultaneously feed and either block or redirect their opponent's movements. Some feeder drills can focus more on attack and counter attack. These ideas can be blended during creative, random free play.

Attacks thrown in combination result in an accumulation of damage, either against a single target or against multiple targets. A jab/cross combo or chain punch sends multiple blows into the same target, increasing the pain. Multiple targets can be selected as well, with each receiving a strong, painful blow impeding the opponent or opponents. Being ready and able to throw consecutive attacks enables us to track a moving opponent effectively, striking him quickly at his next predicted movement or manipulating his movement blow by blow (to maneuver him into a more strategic position).

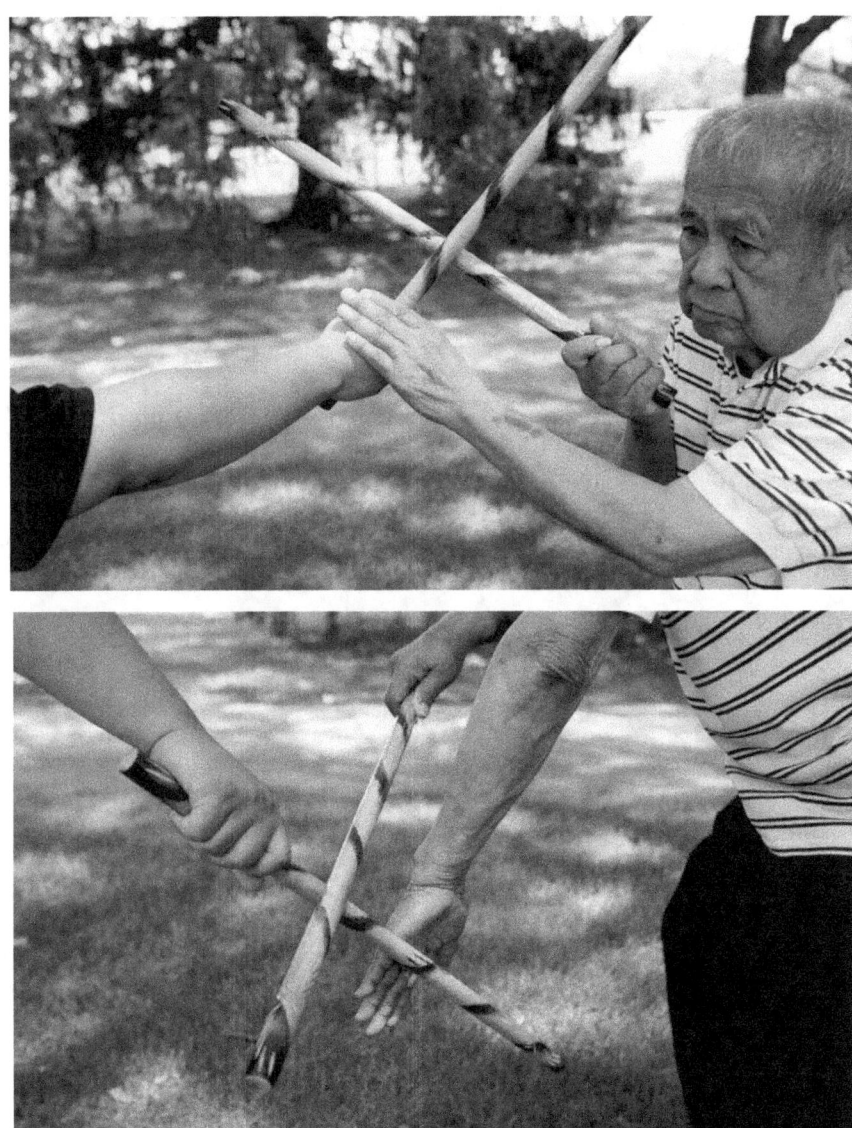

Controls thrown in combination serve more to redirect and maneuver the opponent. Used intelligently and in combination, controls can help limit your opponent's choices of counters, and can lead to restraints and disarms. In any case, the well rounded practitioner employs an intelligent mix of both attacks and controls as necessary, according to each encounter, to achieve his goals.

On Disarms

In our program we consider disarms a low-probability technique. The probability you will need to perform one, the probability that you will successfully perform one, and the probability that you will perform one in reality exactly as you may have rehearsed it in training are all extremely low. Having said that, we do explore the topic to understand how they work.

The most basic disarm already lives in our fundamental five angles. When our opponent attacks, we attack their limb. In most popular Filipino systems this is called "defanging the snake." If the attacking limb is disabled it cannot be used to attack anymore, effectively disarming the opponent. If anyone expresses interest in learning disarms, I always start with this concept of attacking their attack. It is highly effective and relatively simple to execute.

The idea of Filipino weapon disarms conjures images of intricate intertwining of limbs and armaments, ending in a beautiful disarm where the opponent's weapon pops effortlessly out of his hands in mere moments. These demonstrations are beautiful to watch, and can be fascinating explorations into principles of leverage and anatomy, but they are for the most part not a reliable analog of reality. A random, non-compliant opponent simply introduces too many variables to be able to complete a complicated, rehearsed disarmament sequence.

The more important idea is the underlying principles that make a disarm successful. Like the rest of our material, if we understand the core principles, remain physically and mentally fluid, and practice with honest pressure testing, then we can more easily create practical solutions in real time.

The first principle is to *move to safety*. This is basically the same principle from our fundamental footwork and our basics of self-defense. We don't want to stand in one spot and receive an incoming attack if at all possible. In order to gain control of the encounter, we need to proactively move to a position that gives us an advantage. In the tactical world people have called this "getting off the X" or, in other combat systems, simply moving off line. However you want to phrase it, it all means moving.

The next principle we teach is to *control the weapon limb*. After moving to a safer position, we manage the attacking limb to make it more difficult for that limb to harm us. I prefer to grab the whole limb and turn the opponent's body. This is a simple response with bigger muscle groups, and tends to help manage attacks from their other available limbs. Other methods involve entwining the opponent's limb by weaving the sticks into a web of levers, or manipulating the joints of the hand and arm.

Example: Angle 1 Twining Disarm

The last principle of disarming is *applying lateral pressure to the weapon*. We usually have the luxury to apply this only after the previous principles of movement and control have been fulfilled. Lateral pressure works to disarm any weapon, club, blade, even firearm. With enough lateral pressure, eventually every weapon will come out of someone's hand.

What we need to manage while applying this lateral pressure is the danger zones of the weapon involved. Sticks are relatively easy, as motion and pressure are required to create damage. We can simply grab the weapon itself and apply the necessary lateral pressure until the weapon is removed. The potential danger is increased with a blade or firearm, because handling the wrong surface of a blade will result in injury and failure to avoid the danger lines of a firearm can be fatal.

NATURE OF THE WEAPON

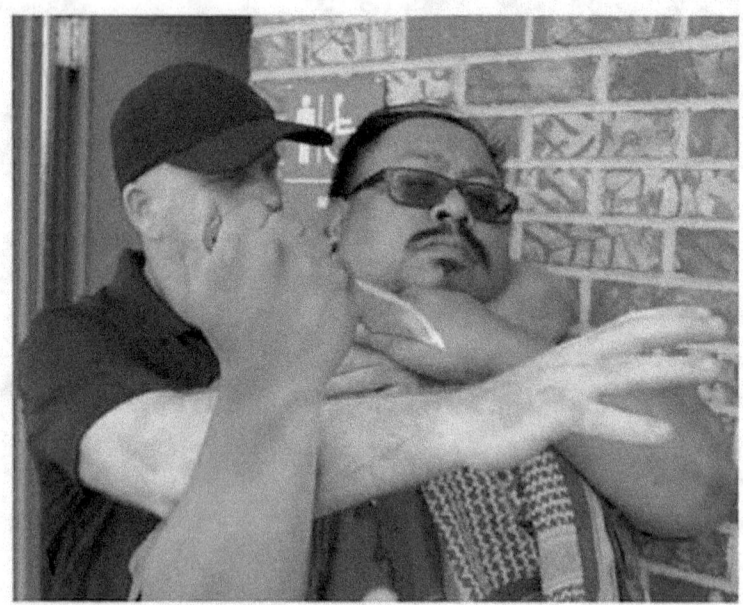

Left: FMA training with a small FMA blade may save your life if you're attacked.

From Knives Illustrated Magazine, October/November 2019

Our primary mode of training is generally with a single stick in the dominant hand, with the remaining hand playing a supporting role that can be either offensive or defensive. Most systems vary in their choice of focus, some preferring longer or shorter sticks or blades, some focusing on the knife, and some preferring a weapon in each hand. The broad overarching principle is that both sides of the body should be as equally capable as possible. Limiting one's training to a single area of focus leaves you unprepared for the possibilities in a random encounter.

I've seen this happen personally, with people trained in, say, primarily double stick becoming awkward and confused when one stick is removed. I've seen initial confusion in my own students when we first transition from stick to knife and new aspects of tool capability and range are revealed. Occasionally I like to confuse them deliberately this way, making them switch hands or weapons, orienting the weapons in a less familiar way to draw out their adaptability.

A game I like to play in class is to grab random weapons from my training bag and analyze their nature. The exercise starts simply enough with the single stick they're holding. What can it do, impact? How can we hit with it? How can we defend? How can we control? How do these aspects change when I change my grip or orientation? You can imagine the options, which is the point. Speaking of points, look now at a knife. It will cut (hi Kuya Doug!)! It will also pierce. Does your particular knife have one edge or two? Is there a curve? Is it designed for a particular orientation in the hand (forward, reverse, edge-in grip, etc.)?

Expanding the game more, we vary our armaments to include stick and knife, single or double blades, axe, karambit, even swords and staffs. With each weapon we discern its nature and capabilities, and we carefully move and play. Regardless of our combination of armaments, we always bring it back to the fundamentals of movement and the framework of our five angles. Basically as we explore the differences we return to the similarities. Regardless of your particular training background, I believe these thought exercises will benefit your practice.

Common Defense Items and Their Usage

While Filipino martial arts is most often associated with the stick and knife, a core value of the art is its ability to weaponize anything you have in your hands in a practical way using the same base of fundamental movements. A skilled FMA practitioner can utilize discarded bottles or shed tree limbs just as effectively for self-defense as a hand-crafted stick or knife. It's a skill meant to transition and adapt, from opponent, to strategy, to armament itself.

Having said that, any specific tool takes practice to use well. Our main training tool in class is the stick, but we branch out and practice with blunt training blades of varying lengths, palm sticks, etc. For students who carry specific tools daily, we usually recommend they acquire an equivalent training tool they can practice with.

Whatever weapon happens to be in your hand, remember to practice retention as well. The capabilities of your tool can be used against you if you're not careful. If it can happen to seasoned violence professionals, it can certainly happen to you. With that, let's look at some common self-defense items.

Stick

This is the main weapon analog we use when training Filipino martial arts. Fortunately, it is also a thing that is common everywhere. While not always clean and uniform like our rattan training sticks, any stick found in nature or civilization can still be used to hit someone, thus creating the pain and space you need to escape to safety. If you choose to deal with the weight and legality of it, you can choose to carry a metal extendable baton. Long sticks, short sticks, me and you sticks, add them to your bag of tricks! Bats and broomsticks, pipes and nightsticks, use them all to hit their… strategic target areas!

Knife

This is a book on Filipino martial arts. Of course I would discuss the knife at some point! Fixed blade or folding, a knife concentrates your mechanical force into its edge and point, producing potentially fight-ending cuts and stabs. Knives come in many shapes, sizes, and configurations depending on their preferred attributes of usage. Want to focus on the point? Need a knife that primarily cuts and slashes? Are you skinning wild game? Does my tool fit my training? If you choose to carry one, pick one that you will willingly carry as a daily habit and spend plenty of practice time drawing and deploying your particular knife. You get bonus points if your particular knife is a useful tool for your everyday life. Be aware of your local laws and ordinances to avoid extralegal difficulty, and remember, a knife is considered lethal force.

Defensive Spray

Defensive sprays are a popular and widely available self-defense tool in the US and various parts of the world. Commercially available spray formulas are capable of inflicting enough pain to stop the average person in their tracks for around a half-hour without causing any permanent harm. Depending on the size of the spray can, you can expect an effective range of 12-15 feet, even 30 feet or more from large bear spray canisters. Of course sprays come with their share of potential disadvantages as well. In windy or enclosed environments, sprays have the potential of blowing or splashing back and affecting the user as well as the attacker. Some spray mechanisms are less intuitive for defensive use. Keep in mind that under threat your fine motor skills begin to deteriorate.

The more steps required to deploy your spray or other defensive tool, the less time you have to act, and your risk rises. If carried in a separate bag or in a glove box, add distance to that complexity and your odds of successful use drop even more. Also, defensive sprays are effective at inflicting pain on the average person. When your attacker is in a chemically altered state, this will affect how they perceive pain, with some people feeling nothing and simply walking through your spicy streams of mist on their way to you. No tool has a record of either total success or zero malfunction. That said, I do highly recommend defensive sprays. Just choose a unit from a company you trust, with a powerful formula that deploys mechanically easily and as precisely as possible, with a generous deployment distance in a size that you will be comfortable carrying daily on your person.

Flashlight

This is one of my favorites because it's useful both for self-defense and for normal everyday life. The light from a flashlight can help you identify potential threats in dark areas and can act as an annoying but harmless deterrent at a distance. Failing that, with the right construction, you can hit someone with it. And unlike some tools, most flashlights will draw no negative scrutiny from law enforcement or security personnel. Today's generation of flashlights have never been smaller or more powerful. You can temporarily blind the scariest of guys in a dark alley and peer down into the darkest of engine bays to find that dipstick or loose bolt, all in a tool that can be small enough to fit in your pocket and carry comfortably every day.

Pen

This is another favorite of mine. Like the flashlight, a pen is something you can easily carry daily and potentially use in normal everyday life. Like a kubaton or knife, it's a tool that focuses your striking power into a smaller point, causing a great deal of pain almost regardless of where it makes contact. And unlike a kubaton or knife, it won't get you in hot water once the law is involved. Almost any pen will do, but I tend to recommend sturdy metal-body pens that will withstand some abuse. Be careful with purpose built "tactical" pens, as the scary points and knurling on some models may again draw negative attention in a legal setting.

Knuckles

This is brass knuckles and various other forms of fist loads with protrusions that support your fist and concentrate your striking force. These can be legally questionable in some areas, and like other tools, may get you in more hot water should you need to use them. If you haven't learned how to safely throw a punch through martial arts or fight sports training, this type of tool can help make up for some of your skill deficit. Some are strong and light enough to keep in a pocket or on a keychain to support a habit of daily carry.

Keys

This is one that gets thrown around the self-defense world a lot. I generally don't recommend using your keys for protection unless you really have no other choice. They are usually difficult to handle, and may cause as much harm to you as to your attacker. Also, if they get damaged during your encounter, your means of escape via vehicle or by locking yourself in your home until help arrives are at risk. If you like the idea of weaponizing your keys, there are products on the market purpose-built to look like keys and fit on your keychain, but that will withstand defensive use.

Firearms

Firearms are a loaded topic, so to speak. In some parts of the world their accessibility is limited and highly regulated. Even the word itself can elicit powerful emotional responses. Whatever your personal ideas are on the topic, the fact remains that firearms, like every other tool listed here, are neutral inanimate objects. The responsibility for their use or abuse falls solely on the person wielding them. Rational people understand this. Firearms are potentially lethal, which makes them an effective deterrent and tool. Anyone inhuman enough to consider criminally victimizing fellow humans may not be swayed by legal repercussions, fines, imprisonment, etc., but most certainly will give pause and reconsider their actions under threat of potential death. The power of the firearm makes it the best choice for populations who are more susceptible to victimization, like the physically smaller, less capable, elderly, or those in positions of inherently higher threat, like law enforcement and military. They are the natural, obvious choice for self-protection. The power of mortality in your hands is a very serious responsibility. While I will never endorse government mandate, expert training in the safe and effective use of a firearm is something I highly and seriously suggest for anyone considering the use of firearms for self-protection.

FOOTWORK

Footwork is taught many ways across martial arts systems. The basic idea behind any good footwork is effective distance management to accomplish your intended goals. Put more simply, my footwork moves me quickly and comfortably to hit someone and to avoid getting hit. This is a loaded topic to say the least, with lifetimes of valuable lessons across systems. Striking systems like karate, the many styles of kung fu, muay thai, boxing etc. carry a lot of lessons about power generation and transmission in their footwork. Grappling systems like judo, wrestling, shuai jiao, etc. teach many lessons about absorbing and redirecting an opponent's force in their footwork. Striking, grappling, and weapon-based arts teach many different lessons about clearing space to approach an opponent very quickly. Good footwork will help you with all of these attributes.

I mentioned earlier that we teach that the feet should move when the hands move. To build coordination and fluidity, we practice this literally for beginners, with one foot moving at the same time as the hands swing the stick: One strike, one step, forward step with forehand strike, backward step with backhand strike. Simple, gross movement. These are the roots of more complex strategic movement. When students grow more comfortable with their coordination I'll often switch reminders to something like "unglue your feet." This serves as a quick reminder that they're overly focused on their opponent's stick, turning the encounter into a standing trade of blows instead of a more thoughtful and fluid exchange.

Lateral movement is the next big footwork idea. It serves the purposes of distance management while also helping mitigate the severity of any incoming attack. Naturally the easiest response to a threat is simply to retreat. In many martial exchanges you will see this pattern of linear advancing and retreating. Think of olympic fencers moving back and forth on the strip (or *"piste"*).

Remember how I said that strikes move inside or outside in relation to your centerline? That also applies to your opponent. Strength and power tend to be most easily applied when your centerline is oriented towards your target. When you're both facing each other squarely, the outcome of that exchange is based more on who has the physical strength advantage. When you move laterally, the opponent has to re-orient their centerline towards you to get the most out of their strikes. When you're lateral to your opponent, you have the advantage and they are at a disadvantage.

ON SELF-DEFENSE

I think that too often the topic of self-defense is presented in a way that is too intimidating, in ways to which the average person doesn't relate. When we hear the term self-defense, we tend to imagine pro fighters, mma champions, military special forces, or law enforcement professionals.

The reality is that self-defense is and should be for everyone! You don't have to have the body of a Greek god, or have black belts in multiple martial arts systems. I think we should start by considering three general concepts that the average everyday person should relate to, that will help on the path to personal safety. Those concepts are Personal Responsibility, Health & Condition, and Objective Honesty.

Personal Responsibility is the reality that you alone are responsible for yourself. Ultimately no one else bears the responsibility for your safety, health, education, and training. I always hear people talk about "just calling the cops" (ironically, at this point in history people are simultaneously crying out to "defund the police"). The truth is that no cop will ever arrive in time to protect you from immediate danger. You need to understand and accept the cold hard fact that you are responsible for yourself.

Health & Condition relates to your body and mind. To quote renowned strength coach Mark Rippetoe, "Strong people are harder to kill than weak people and more useful in general." A physically strong and healthy body is always more resistant to all forms of harm, and is more capable of executing effective techniques. And a healthier mind can handle unexpected stress and make better decisions.

What tempers everything else is a firm grasp and free application of Objective Honesty. This helps us understand the realities of human violence, the truth about our personal health and condition, and the defensive concepts and techniques we choose to train.

Without a healthy dose of Objective Honesty, we can become trapped in a fantasy bubble, imagining ourselves the hero of our own cheesy action movie, with scores of enemies falling unconscious at our slightest touch. It's a fun thought, but it gets us nowhere.

There's a lot of information out there, and not all of it is good. But these three concepts of Personal Responsibility, Health & Condition, and Objective Honesty will definitely help guide you. There is no downside for martial artists to learn more about self-defense. I encourage you to find quality resources on this topic and study further.

Violence & Personal Responsibility

Whenever we encounter violence in nature, it is almost always exclusively predatory. Whether it's wolves, big cats, sharks stalking prey animals, or invasive vines slowly choking their host trees of nutrition and sunlight, nature is full of examples of life taking advantage of other life for the sake of resources.

The field of human violence can be a lifetime study all its own. In practical terms for the martial artist and teacher, let me simplify the topic. Predators don't behave like rational human beings, and can't be dealt with rationally. What this means is that any person who is in a state of mind where they justify or even seek out violence against another human being is no longer abiding by the comfortable rules of society that you're used to. Like beer goggles that afflict the late-night bar-going crowd, human predators are looking at the world through totally different eyes from you. If put in a position to deal with one, we need to understand how they see the world.

A human predator can have several end goals for his violence, like his animal counterpart. He may be out to gain property, assert his dominance to his tribe, or simply to enjoy the violence. We can think of clear examples of each of these. A mugger threatens people for their money or possessions. A carjacker attempts to steal cars. Sexual predators seek physical gratification. Gang members or other group predators may commit violence against people to gain status in their group. A serial killer seeks gratification through the death of others. All of these layers of violence exist in the world, and any honest martial arts teacher wanting to prepare their students to face the possibility of this violence should learn, understand, and honestly present at least the fundamentals of this knowledge to his students.

Safety from predators comes from power, both individually and collectively. Hyenas and lions have an antagonistic relationship in the wild. Lions are, to most cultures, a symbol of strength and power. They are not often harassed by hyenas unless they are alone. Emboldened by their numbers, they may begin to threaten a solitary lion, and may pay dearly for overextending themselves. However, the lion too can call upon its own collective power, the rest of its pride, to come to its aid. And so can we! The first strategy, certainly one that will appeal to the martial artist, is to become a bigger, stronger, more capable animal, a harder target. Predators across species have a distaste for expending too much time and too many calories on difficult prey.

We see the other self-protection strategy in herds of herbivores. Solitary animals under attack by predators will run for their lives with everything they have until they either succumb to their attackers, outrun the threat, or rejoin the safety of the herd where the most powerful members can provide some defense. As a human animal in human society, our approach will be some of both. Anyone can learn to be a harder target. At the same time we can also learn how to escape quickly and leverage the power of the crowd as much as possible.

Simply put, when individuals take personal responsibility for their preparedness and safety, the community becomes safer. I don't believe this should be mandated by law or anything like that. Ultimately the more empowered and educated each individual person can become, the safer the overall community can be. And in my opinion, a healthy dose of the classic "golden rule" can make this safer community a bit more pleasant.

Layers of Safety - Basic Avoidance and De-Escalation

We manage our personal safety with several zones of action: observation, communication, and physical. We discuss them separately but they always work simultaneously in practice. Self-defense encounters rarely occur without warning or pretext, though some victims may feel blindsided. They likely feel this way because they neglected our first layer of safety: observation.

Observation is simply your awareness of the environment around you, and your educated choices based on that information. Down the road we see a shady street corner with several stereotypical ruffians eyeing the passing pedestrians. Do we choose to keep walking right into them, or maybe find a different route? That's observation.

Our next layer of safety, communication, has a bit more girth. This layer actually begins visually with what you communicate through your body language. Someone who is alert and confident communicates a different message to observers than someone who is inattentive and frightened. Experienced predators will pick up on body language quickly while evaluating their potential targets. If this concept is new or unfamiliar to you, I suggest having a friend take a video of you walking around town one day so you can see how you carry yourself in public. If you look like someone you think would be easily victimized, you can begin working on building a more empowered physical presence.

The other aspect of communication in a self-defense context is verbal communication. Simply put, this is where we use our words. There is certainly some nuance to this, as the wrong tone of voice in a particular circumstance may turn an encounter sour. The general points that will help you most are to be loud enough to hear, and clear with your choice of words and intent.

First, you ensure that someone threatening you can hear and understand what you want. A confident, audible "Stop!" may be enough to get your point across. It may not actually stop the encounter, but it begins to establish boundaries. It also begins to alert anyone in the general public nearby to your location and circumstances. If things do escalate to the physical, any bystanders already alerted to your encounter may begin to be witnesses, or may take a more active role and step in or call law enforcement. In today's culture some people may simply stand on the sidelines and take video on their phones for entertainment value, but this is at least some way of reaching out for herd safety.

Again, tone and word choice can affect the outcome of your encounter. A "Please stop" or "Back off" will be seen differently in court than saying, "Come any closer and I'll kill you!" We want to avoid a physical altercation in the first place if possible, and potential legal hassle if it comes to that. When we train this in my classes we start by putting up our open hands, stepping a foot back, and practicing saying a loud, firm "Stop." This way we practice both our body language and our verbal communication in a simple, repeatable way.

The absolute last resort, and the last layer of safety, is physical. This is the part at which, despite your best efforts to avoid trouble, someone is determined to exploit you and their attack has already begun. Now you must use enough physical force and technique in order to create space and escape back to safety. Remember we're not training to win a trophy or a title belt in these instances. We don't need to go for a knockout or tapout. There's no referee to step in when things get too rough, and there are no rules to worry about breaking. The goal is NOT to defeat or subdue your attacker. That's law enforcement's job. Your job is not to be in danger anymore.

You must use everything and anything in your power to create physical space between you and the source of danger, then escape to safety. In the case of escaping an attacker, this can mean moving towards a secure place like the safety of a locked room or a well-lit public place with more people to remove the advantage of your attacker's privacy. Running aimlessly is bad and could lead you to more danger. Ideally while you were observing your environment, part of you is thinking about safe places to escape to if necessary. Under stress, you may just have to follow the lights.

Legal Issues

Regardless of the outcome of an encounter, you will always have to deal with the legal system. You will be faced with law enforcement and criminal court, and even possibly civil court. Often your time dealing with the law will far outlast the length of time spent surviving your defensive encounter. A close friend of mine survived a sexual assault and attempted murder. Even though the suspect was apprehended in a miraculously short amount of time, and even with overwhelming evidence in her favor, her family still had to endure years of court proceedings at the hands of the suspect's defense lawyers. Thankfully that particular monster has been locked away for what is essentially a life sentence, but the fact remains that even a seemingly clear-cut case can cost you and your family agonizing time and a small fortune. Do what's necessary to survive violence, but remember, inappropriate use of force will work against you. Create a good relationship with a quality lawyer in case the need arises.

Basic Health and Fitness

545 lb (247 kg) Sumo Deadlift in Birkenstock Sandals & Torn Cargo Pants

Physical Capability

I feel that it's important to acknowledge the importance of your physical health and capability in any discussion about self-defense and martial arts. Some people seem to think that physical condition is largely less relevant compared to martial skill or technique. I would agree that excellent technique skillfully applied with excellent timing against a compromised opponent can yield results that appear magical. And I will never suggest that you do not pursue your martial disciplines to the deepest extent possible through a lifetime of thoughtful study and practice. But we should be open and honest about the benefits of a strong, healthy, capable body driving your techniques.

At this point in history I've heard many traditional systems talk about the importance of structure, connection, leverage, timing etc. while denouncing any form of physical development outside of their system's accepted practices. Stereotypes about reduced capability from being too "muscle-bound" persist even now despite an abundance of evidence otherwise. An often blind, fanatical faith in ideas of mysterious universal energies fuels the worst kind of overconfidence in the most vulnerable of people, typically leading them into great disappointment at the very least. At most, it brings them to physical harm.

I'm certainly not advising that everyone who has an interest in personal safety should become a professional strongman or Olympian. But you have to admit, it's a lot harder to create space and escape to safety when you start breathing heavily after half a flight of steps and you're carrying around fifty pounds of extra insulation. Barring any major structural damage or organ failures, the average person can increase their overall health and defensive capability with a relatively simple minimum daily investment of time and effort.

The most basic principle is simply to *move*. Move every day. If nothing else, find some kind of movement you enjoy and do it with enough consistency and intensity to make you sweat a little that day. Repeat. If your starting point is being completely sedentary, daily sweat that you enjoy is a good thing.

If you want to develop yourself from there, a good next step is "push, pull, squat." You can fulfill each of these simple directives with an immense variety of exercise variations, ranging from bodyweight calisthenics to the use of weights, bands, and other equipment. However you fulfill them, push, pull, and squat effectively exercise the whole body. We're not focusing on building you huge pecs or biceps here. The goal is to make your whole body more useful, more capable, and healthier in the process.

Again, if you're starting from sedentary, just start moving. From there, you can start a simple daily routine of bodyweight calisthenics that involve the push, pull, and squat. In our classes we will often warm up with three to five rounds of whole-body circuits, performing ten repetitions each of some version of push-ups, squats, sit-ups, and pull-ups or band pulls, with a brief rest between rounds. This ensures a comprehensive whole-body workout for almost all our students, from children to adults and even seniors. It's a fairly simple, comprehensive protocol that you can perform daily. As long as your form is correct, you will enjoy minimal risk of injury and increase your overall health relatively quickly.

The options for physical development begin to expand as your general condition improves. Or, as some readers may discover, their employment or circumstances require greater or more specific physical capabilities of them. Military, law enforcement, and security professionals often have protocols set by their respective agencies. People seeking to become competitive combat athletes likewise have specialized protocols and facilities accessible to them to meet those goals. Regardless of environment or goals, I tend to favor and suggest to people to engage in a quality strength training program, usually based again on the simple push, pull, squat idea. The strength and power one develops from even a simple program based on these compound lifts has immense benefits to every other aspect of one's martial and athletic pursuits.

Here I must specify "strength and power" training, which is distinctly different from and often confused with "bodybuilding." While good strength and power training can and does build muscle mass while increasing performance, the whole goal of bodybuilding is to develop muscle mass towards a certain physical appearance for the competitive stage. The mass developed in the sport of bodybuilding is often not useful for other forms of work, nor is your overall health and nutrition ideal for daily function. In fact, most people don't realize that for people to look "ripped" and "cut" on stage or screen, they must literally starve and dehydrate themselves to maintain that appearance for a precious small window of time. When the competition is done and the last picture or video is taken, these poor people are left exhausted, their carefully restricted nutrition plans cast aside for relief binging, increasing the risk for a whole new set of problems.

Equating bulges, veins, and striations with overall health is incorrect and unhealthy. I always advise training for performance as opposed to appearance. If weight loss is a necessary part of your path to better health, it should be done cautiously, intelligently, and sustainably while supporting your level of athletic activity. There's already volumes of excellent material on the topics of nutrition, weight loss, strength, power development, and more.

Some starting advice is simply to record everything you eat and drink in a day. Knowledge is power, right? If you notice a trend of boxes of snack cakes and cases of soft drinks, you have some idea of what to change. Maybe drink more water and replace some of those snack cakes with a fruit or vegetable or five. Be informed, start simply, and make sustainable progress. Going too hard, too fast in either nutrition or training will result in regression and injury, without question.

Basic Nutrition

I want to talk a little bit about diet. Weight loss is a recurring topic in the realm of martial arts and fitness in general. Often people get overwhelmed by the sheer volume of information out there. My goal is to help you narrow your focus a little and grasp some basic concepts that will help you achieve your health and nutrition goals, whatever they are.

Example: Delicious Chicken Wings

No Food Is Bad

Please avoid moralizing diets. It's unhealthy for your mind and eventually it will be unhealthy for your body as well. Often some foods and even whole food groups earn a bad reputation. Things like fat and salt, and more recently carbohydrates, have been considered unhealthy according to "common knowledge." Remember, everything has its purpose in the right proportions. Carbs, fats, salts, etc. all have some positive nutritional role. Often, problems arise from carelessly cutting those things out of one's diet. "The dose makes the poison!" In turn, there is no one single "superfood" or supplement that will cure all your ills all by itself! Sorry, guys, but that solitary salad and multivitamin won't balance out your entire crave case of cheesy greaseburgers.

What Are Your Goals, Really?

I've worked with volumes of people over the years now who claim their goals are one thing or another, but they turn out to be entirely appearance-based. Or, when given the answer to their stated issue, they immediately disagree because of some gross misinformation or some contrary ideas that come from a different set of goals. You will need to do some work and find the best balance for you. Do you want to lose fat, gain energy, gain mass? Do you need to support your martial arts or other athletic activity? What is your current condition? If you're unsure about this, go see your doctor and get your bearings. Ask yourself: Realistically, what are your limitations? Commonly these have something to do with the amount of time and money you have to work with. The more honest and clear you are with your goals, current condition, and limitations, the easier it will be to plan your direction and take action.

Giordano's Chicago Style Pizza

Small Changes, Long Game

Once you know where you're going, remember: small changes are easier and add up over time. We're playing the long game! Start by adding better things to your diet. Again, I'm not moralizing food. I just mean food that's better for meeting your nutritional goals. Adding items of high nutritional value like spinach, carrots, bell peppers, and Greek yogurt will start moving the needle in the right direction. For more information on high value nutrition for athletes, you can check out the *Vertical Diet* by renowned trainer Stan Efferding.

Add Better First, Remove Worse Later

As you add better things, gradually remove worse things. When your guts are full of extra servings of vegetables and water at each meal, there's that much less room for food or drinks that may work against your goals. The easiest elements to start removing are liquid calories (soft drinks, juice boxes, gallons of beer etc.) and processed convenience foods. Often these foods cut nutritional corners for the sake of convenience and taste. Plan to meal prep and prepare to adjust the proportions according to your goals.

Finishing 10 Consecutive Lobsters in Halifax, Nova Scotia

Lateral Positive Changes

Something we might not immediately think of is to make lateral positive changes. While you gradually adjust your diet, why not clean your room or work space? Maybe take some more short walks through the day, or even take some daily minutes to meditate. We're playing the long game, changing habits and crafting a new lifestyle!

Taking A German Sign Literally

Accept Occasional Indulgence

Having said all that, don't forget to indulge occasionally! New habits take time to build. Your body needs time to adjust. Huge, cold-turkey life changes aren't for everyone, and often that approach backfires. Social life is also part of your health. Don't be that one friend who HAS to have something special to eat or drink when you go out, or you may be invited less.

ON TEACHING

I want to give some value to my colleagues who are instructors at their own schools, but may not have extensive experience in the field of education. I have a bachelor's degree in education, and at the point of writing this book, just about twenty years of experience in education and childcare. Everyone teaches differently, but I wanted to share some of my thoughts. I hope it helps!

Be Concise

This is more true the younger your students are. You may be excited about your body of knowledge. You could probably speak for hours on the depths of your art with your fellow instructors. But I guarantee you the kids in your classes barely have the attention span to look directly in your eyes for five seconds in a row. Figure out the shortest, easiest way to communicate effectively whatever you're working on. Adult novices are very similar. They're already taking a big step by taking your class in the first place. If you flood them immediately with decades of your hard-earned knowledge, it may scare them right back out the door. Be concise!

Scale Appropriately

Having said that, be prepared to scale appropriately. Some students and certain circumstances will start to lead quickly into deeper waters. Don't be afraid to discuss deeper or more complicated concepts when the appropriate opportunity arises. Be ready to adapt quickly!

Be Clear

This, of course, ties in to being concise, but it goes beyond curriculum into the daily operation of your classes. Clear goals help students focus on the individual class day and their long-term goals. Belt systems are a form of clarity for students. By organizing curriculum into progressive stages, it gives students an idea of what they've done and where they're going.

Clear boundaries and expectations help keep everyone safe and help avoid potential problems during training. Signals like the "tap" or clear safe words like "stop" are clear and easy to understand.

Instructors should develop clear communication skills, both verbal and non-verbal. Nobody learns well when they can't understand you. Don't mumble!

Consider Tone

Consider your tone with people. Not everyone is prepared for the old-school drill instructor style of training. Nor does everyone appreciate a condescending tone, especially not kids! Speak loudly and clearly, with respect and clarity. Be genuine, listen carefully, be understanding, and respond thoughtfully. You'll avoid a lot of problems!

Be Confident

In my experience, I've found that students prey on weakness. They require strength to give and earn respect. I'm not saying to be cruel or mean. But if you exhibit self-doubt, your students will think twice about accepting anything you're trying to teach them. Confidence!

Be An Expert

Even the newest, most green new teacher usually knows more than their students. Be confident in your knowledge and constantly seek to improve yourself. Students will accept an honest "I don't know", but will eat you alive if you pretend to know more than you really do. Know your limits!

Be Prepared and Organized

Know your general plan for class, have whatever equipment you need already prepped, and you'll avoid dead time. Dead time leads to distraction, which can leave you expending more energy to help everyone refocus. Your students are paying you for an education. When you willingly allow for more distraction, you're basically stealing time and value from your students. Distractions happen, but don't make them a habit!

Be Aware

You can't deal with issues that you don't notice! Besides, the more you practice active awareness in a teaching context, the more you can bring this skill to bear in other contexts like self-defense or combat.

Pick Your Battles

If you're fortunate, your class is full of students, each with their own issues to work on. If you spend too much time on any one student, you're not serving the rest of your students well. Pick and choose which issues to address and when. If you're thoughtful, you can find a way to address the entire class and cover several issues at once.

This principle is for your own well-being too. You have only so much energy and attention in a day. If you don't budget yourself wisely, you'll end up burning yourself out on a minor point, and become less valuable to your students for the rest of that class. Remember, martial arts is a long game, so choose your battles wisely!

Be Patient

Your students haven't been training as long as you have. Nor are they nearly as interested and excited in the topic as you are. They can't be, they just started! Not to mention, depending on how young your students are, you're literally fighting their biology! Double down on your meditation or something. Just find a way to develop your patience.

Repeat and Reinforce

A classic principle used in politics, media, and religion through the ages, for better or worse (often worse), is to repeat and reinforce. Be ready to say the same things repeatedly! When you say something that helps your students understand and improve, be ready to say it again. It will remind those students of things to improve, and it will potentially help your new students learn and understand things more quickly and easily.

Verbalize Learning

Martial arts is heavily physical. However, when you can verbally explain what's happening, the learning happens more deeply. And it usually helps you as the instructor to understand your material more deeply as well!

Don't Take Things Too Personally

You and your students are all human, presumably. You'll all make mistakes and have moments when you are not at your best. Be patient and understanding with them, and they'll be more likely to return the courtesy, and maybe less likely to find another place to train!

Foster Independence and Personal Responsibility

However you structure your martial arts experience, you are there to facilitate each student's individual martial arts journey. You and the parents can do only so much for them. The best we can do to help students get the most from their time on the mats is to teach them how to be personally responsible for their training. If they look to you for every little thing, if the students can't do anything without you, I would argue that you've created a cult, not a healthy martial arts school. They need opportunity to exercise their individual thinking skills at least as much as they get to exercise their bodies in class. They need to be allowed to make mistakes and to learn from these mistakes. They need to learn to question you respectfully, and you need to learn to set aside any pride or hubris to respond respectfully.

SELECTING A SCHOOL

Choosing a school is a big and sometimes scary choice. I hope these ideas help.

The first question is simple. Do you like the school? Some places you walk in and it just feels right! Students and teachers seem happy, the facilities and equipment look safe and fun, and the teaching is easy to understand and effective. These are not the only things to consider when you're deciding on a school, but they're important.

Another thing to consider is the money. Good programs cost money, but you must find what works for you. No program is worth extra debt or financial distress. Just like the other aspects of your budget, don't do anything you can't afford.

Martial arts mastery is a long-term commitment. Having said that, I suggest trying to avoid long term contracts if you're not comfortable with them. These were more popular years ago, and if you're definitely committed to train at a particular school for at least one to three years, it may even save you some money. But remember, life happens and your plans may change. Getting out of a long contract may create more hassle than you're willing to deal with. Schools today should be able to offer you other options. If you're not comfortable, be open and honest. If a school tries to bully you into something you're not comfortable with, say "good day" and walk out the door. There are other programs out there.

Choosing a style you like is important, but one of the most important things to look for is good teachers. They should have a history of quality training, a length of teaching experience that you respect, and a clean criminal history (or at least a thorough and proven history of reformation that you are willing to accept, *caveat emptor*). A good teacher should be honest and straightforward about all of these things, and should be fine with you double checking their credentials.

Even when you find excellent teachers whom you respect, you shouldn't blindly trust ANY teacher. Remember, you're still responsible for your family and their safety. Good teachers are assets, but never replacements for you!

FAMILY ANECDOTES

Dad actually tried teaching people his Filipino martial arts back in the 1970s, before I was born. His main frustration was that his American students "can't move their hands and feet." Later on when I began to teach, I discovered the truth of his statement. Much like dance, new students tend to lack the coordination between their hands and feet to move comfortably and fluidly. This helped fuel my continuous mission to learn more and better ways to communicate to broader audiences. If this sounds like you, consider dancing lessons.

Grandma Anita & Grandpa Silvino

Dad recounts various Filipino styles he's encountered over the years, usually with interesting and unexpected practical lessons for me. For instance, a double weapons practitioner (double cudgel sinawali, as dad puts it) came to dad's gym back in the Philippines. The man said it was embarrassing and unjustifiable to walk around downtown with two bolos on, one on each hip, so he came to train single stick with dad.

Another encounter was a duel with two bladed men around mom's village. They were both playing very offensively in what amounted to a blow for blow exchange. One man was stabbed in the gut, and immediately he stabbed the other man in the gut. One man cast a cut to the head, and so did the other. Even as blood and entrails began spilling out of both men, they persisted in their mutual attacks. Against a more defensive opponent this may gain you some ground, but with both playing the same strategy it ends up being a slaughterhouse.

I've often asked Dad if anyone else in the family besides he and Grandpa knew or taught any martial arts. The answer is a little sad, but not surprising. The handful of his other brothers who learned any martial arts material were largely secretive about it. Uncle Eufemio was allegedly quite skilled with stick and knife, but refused to share any of his knowledge for fear of it being used against him. Unfortunately, like many, he took whatever skill and knowledge he had to his grave.

I'm told Grandpa's brother on Dad's side was a specialist in long cane. By his description, it was a heavy hitting style which often employed retreating attacks. The blade used by his Spanish rebellion counterparts was stored over the shoulder, and was so long it had to be placed on the ground in order to unsheathe it. A cut from a blade like that would have been devastating.

Many of Dad's other siblings were simply interested in other things, like music, foreign sports and martial arts, wooing ladies etc. Some of my cousins were caught up in the ninja craze of the 1980s, choosing to don their black headbands and sneak and leap about town. My own ninja craze of the time involved genetically modified violent reptiles.

He describes the outlook on Filipino martial arts back then as a popular game or sport around the farms. It seems, at least in his region, it wasn't always viewed with the reverential awe or mystique that other martial arts systems enjoy. This is a trend I've seen throughout an increasingly westernized modern Asia, as newer generations become enamored by the exotic cultural offerings of the rest of the world. I don't think it's bad, but it always has a cost. If we're not careful, elements of cultural heritage around the world risk being forgotten. I feel like I'm doing my small part by committing my information to this book.

The View From Mom's Old Farm In Pangasinan

Back: Frank Delo Sr., Frank Delo Jr., Tita G. Delo
Front: Martha & Miguel Gabanit

While this book is mostly about the material I received from Dad, I did get a little knowledge from my late mother's dad, Tatay Miguel. Mom's side of the family is from Pangasinan. Tatay Miguel was a World War II veteran, and would occasionally share stories of his guerilla battles against invading Japanese soldiers. I very clearly remember him bringing a knife home that he found on a fishing trip, and explaining to me in great detail the process of knifing a sentry in the subclavian artery from behind. Fascinating information to bestow on a seven year old. I'm sure my elementary teachers were thrilled to hear all about it.

Dad's 85th birthday, September 17, 2021

Dad describes the barrio he grew up in and the surrounding mountain countryside like a veritable Eden. He tells me stories of the lush tropical forests, rich with an amazing array of seasonal fruits, streams and rivers with cool delicious fresh water, teeming with fresh-water fish that you could eat straight from the water if you wanted. He recalls his mother preparing and preserving portions of this natural bounty to enjoy through the year, with recipes and methods unfortunately lost to time. He spoke of days, and sometimes nights, as a young boy riding his carabao, building an early reputation for brazen courage and playful mischief around the countryside. It's a touching recollection that set my own young imagination ablaze. I wondered what it would be like to run free around those forests. I imagined myself in my late grandmother's kitchen, anticipating the enjoyment of some mystery dishes made from nature's miracles and generations of care. I longed to taste and smell the Philippines of my father's youth.

When I was a bit older, and perhaps more prepared to bear the disappointment, Dad told me the fate of that boyhood paradise. Indeed, if home were such an idyll, why leave to come to the United States in the first place? Sadly, the elements of that bountiful wilderness drew more attention than they could sustain. The fertile fruit trees were stripped bare, their fruit long gone, their wood harvested to fulfill some distant use. The fresh water was picked clean of its fish, its water diverted to larger industrial farming operations. Eventually the erosion filled in the surrounding bodies of water, making the area more prone to mudslides. Dad left Eden behind, and when he returned years later to bury his father, he returned to an eroded dirt field. The family he left behind chose modern distractions and temporary comforts over the heritage of responsible agriculture and their legacy of the land.

Frank Delo Jr. & Friend Ken Visiting The Philippines in the 1990's

Eventually as a teenager I visited the farm homes of both my dad and mom in their respective provinces in the Philippines. It was all still quite tropical and exotic to me, a fluffy American son born to first-generation immigrants. The greatest hardships I had suffered growing up were when my original Nintendo Game Boy ran out of batteries, or I was too late to catch the passing ice cream truck.

My parents lived lives of hard farm labor and put themselves through college, mom in nursing (of course), and dad in criminal justice. Through that hard work and education, they forged a life for our family that their ancestors could only dream of. Our modest suburban home was a palace in comparison to the literal huts in my parents' villages. The relative convenience of the average American grocery store was a kingly bounty, compared to a life of sweat and blood to harvest precious calories from the Earth. Seeing where my family came from made me forever appreciate the quality of life we have here in the United States. I sincerely hope that the Philippines of today can learn and grow from its past, to create a present and a future where the best of Dad's boyhood paradise can live on for future generations.

Dad's US law enforcement career

Dad told me about one of his martial arts students in the Philippines. They were practicing weapon disarms from judo, and his student was learning the techniques well and growing bolder and more confident. For the most part they were using blunt wooden training weapons for practice. But on the day of his student's rank promotion, dad drew a polished (and blunt, unknown to the student) steel blade and attacked him. The bold, confident disarm he had performed probably hundreds of times before with the wooden toy knives had disappeared, replaced instead by frantic retreat. That was my first introduction to the ideas of combat stress management and the dangers of false confidence.

Dad always had a funny, sometimes infuriating mix of both humility and pride. He isn't a blowhard by any means, or at least I've never known him to be one. He's always been an observant, caring teacher, both to me growing up, and to his martial arts students over the years. Where Mom would be white-knuckling the passenger door when I was behind the wheel with my learner's permit, Dad would simply offer timely reminders of the essentials. There is always an element of trust as he teaches, which I appreciate and try to emulate in my own education work.

The infuriating part is when he'll be reminded of something and just casually bring up a heretofore unmentioned but incredibly awesome part of his past, leaving me with more questions than before. For instance, when we started subleasing space for the martial arts school in our local Masonic Temple building, he casually mentioned that he used to be a high ranking Mason years ago, but he got tired of paying dues so he just quit. You can imagine my shock at discovering my dad was part of a secret society. Or when offering him help one day with a broken light fixture, he casually mentioned that he apprenticed as an electrician, then proceeded to wire everything up and bolt everything down unassisted and without incident. This may not move the needle for some, but he is well into his 80s at this point.

Perhaps you may be thinking that Dad's just pulling my leg, that maybe he just enjoys screwing around with his son's little brain. I'm sure he would, but these moments are plentiful throughout my lifetime, and each time Dad has nothing to gain by telling me these things. I was told by an older cousin that Dad literally dodged bullets and disarmed a man while on duty as a police officer. I thought that was the coolest thing I had ever heard, but for my entire lifetime up to that point, Dad had never breathed a word of that occasion to me. Maybe he didn't want to endanger me by making me think that was extra cool and pursuing my own career in law enforcement. When I asked Dad about this story, all he said to me is that he just watched where the guy's gun was pointing and tried to avoid it. He also complained that a fellow officer took the credit for that victory when the reporters showed up. I hope that person gets what he deserves from the universe.

Overall I learned to live a cool, satisfying life without feeling obliged to seek validation for it from anyone. Those moments, when they arise in conversation, can be special treats for the right people at the right time.

Acknowledgments

Thanks to my father Frank, who humored me in my interest in learning his farm games long enough to share their value with the world.

Thanks to my late mother Tita, whose love and lessons persist beyond your earthly time with us.

Thanks to my students at Amalgam Martial Academy, and everyone else who entrusted some portion of their safety and well-being to our instruction.

Thanks to my editor Phil Elmore for your expertise, advice, and hard work.

You all helped make this dream a reality. I am forever grateful.

Suggested Resources

There is a world full of excellent resources for your personal development. This is not a comprehensive list by any means. But I hope the listed resources here give you a good head start. And many of these authors have multiple works that may prove invaluable to you. Enjoy!

Faber, Adele, and Elaine Mazlish. How to Talk so Kids Can Learn: At Home and in School ; What Every Parent and Teacher Needs to Know. Scribner, 2003.

Larkin, Tim. When Violence Is the Answer: Learning How to Do What It Takes When Your Life Is at Stake. Little, Brown and Company, 2017

McNamara, Patrick. Sentinel: Become The Agent in Charge of Your Own Protection Detail. IUniverse, 2012

Miller, R. K. Facing violence: Preparing for the unexpected: Ethically, emotionally, physically (... and without going to prison). YMAA Publication Center, 2011

Rippetoe, Mark. Starting Strength: Basic Barbell Training, 3rd edition. The Aasgaard Company, 2011

Roberts, Chris. Disarm Daily Conflict: Your Life Depends On It. Chris Roberts, 2020

Wiley, Mark V. Mastering Eskrima Disarms. Tambuli Media, 2013

AUTHOR BIO

Frank Delo Jr. has spent most of his life doing a number of things that are not in any way nursing, to the shock and dismay of some fellow Filipinos. Instead he has completely wasted his time performing music around the world and teaching students from age three to ninety-plus the joys and benefits of music and the martial arts.

Frank shares his value with the world from his incredibly secret fortress somewhere in the greater Chicagoland area. Come share his fascinating and completely non-nursing-related content at AmalgamMartialAcademy.com, ClarinetDojo.com, and Midwest Knife and Tool on Facebook and Instagram.

Love this book? Don't forget to leave a review!

Every review matters, and it matters a *lot!*

Head over to Amazon or wherever you purchased this

book to leave an honest review for me.

Maraming salamat po (thank you)!

www.ingramcontent.com/pod-product-compliance
Lightning Source LLC
Chambersburg PA
CBHW070708130626
46553CB00005B/1896